New Kid on the Block

An Easy Reference Guide For Supervisors and Managers

by

Dafna Vann-Gauthier

This book is for first line supervisors, veteran supervisors, managers, leaders, and interim supervisors

authorHOUSE®

2-26-14
Lori,
Thank you for being a part of the CDSB team!
Mary Brunner

AuthorHouse™
1663 Liberty Drive, Suite 200
Bloomington, IN 47403
www.authorhouse.com
Phone: 1-800-839-8640

AuthorHouse™ UK Ltd.
500 Avebury Boulevard
Central Milton Keynes, MK9 2BE
www.authorhouse.co.uk
Phone: 08001974150

First published by AuthorHouse 12/3/2007

ISBN: 978-1-4343-1541-0 (sc)
ISBN: 978-1-4343-1541-0 (sc)

Printed in the United States of America
Bloomington, Indiana

This book is printed on acid-free paper.

New Kid on the Block offers positive techniques and tools to assist individuals in becoming effective managers. It offers an array of basic skills and guidelines to assist managers in their leadership roles. Whether you are just beginning to supervise or have been at it for a long time, this book is a good way to ensure that your supervisory skills are up to date with today's work force. It offers a wealth of knowledge and insight that you can apply to your work situations.

I hope each and every one of you who read this book will get something from it.

Sincerely,
Dafna

My first book is dedicated to my children, Jazzlynn, Joshua, and Breana. To let them know that anything is possible. You can achieve any dream you wish to fulfill if you put your mind to it. And to my parents LaVerne Easter and George Vann (deceased), for teaching me I can do anything possible.

Thank You.

This Book Will Teach You

- The Role of a Supervisor
- How to avoid the Most Common mistakes made by supervisors
- How to create your own leadership style
- How to build a better workplace for your employees
- How to set goals with your employees
- Team Building: Getting employees involved
- Techniques to gain support from your staff when it comes to changes
- How to make employees feel positive change vs. negative
- How to make employees feel like intrapreneurs in your organization
- The meaning and definition of corporate culture, values, beliefs, and mission statements
- How to incorporate corporate culture, values, beliefs, and mission statements into your organization
- Samples of performance appraisals, attendance evaluations, documented counseling, and much more!

BEING PROMOTED

Congratulations! You have been promoted to your new position. You are the new boss in charge, or also known to others as, "**The New Kid on the Block**". You have new responsibilities, a new role, and a new leadership title. Well, what does it all mean? What do you do first? How do you get started? How can you adjust into your new role?

Transitioning into your new role comes with many responsibilities. As a manager, you will need to plan, organize, monitor, and lead your staff in the direction that the organization is heading. You will wear many hats that will encompass your daily activities. The hats you will wear will consist of a decision maker, problem solver, delegator, counselor, evaluator, motivator, communicator, technical expert, disciplinarian, coach, and mentor-should I say more? Making a transition into your new position can be exciting, yet challenging. However, making the right transition can be critical. The skills and tools this book has to offer will guide you to an easier transition in your new role then most who have not read this book.

Managers today must have a variety of skills to be successful. As the new person in charge, the first thing you want to do is identify your role. Your role will be to manage the workforce and carry out the goals of the organization.

In order to do this, managers must be able to perform the management functions of planning, organizing, controlling, and leading the work of others.

Setting forth **plans** to reach the goals of the organization should be a task that all managers should possess. Planning is key to organizational success. It is stated if you fail to plan, you plan to fail. Having some type of plan or road map of what you would like to accomplish as a manager will help direct yourself and staff in the direction the organization is heading.

Another management function that will assist yourself and staff is having structure within your organization. Providing an **organizational** chart will allow employees the opportunity to understand the configuration of the organization. Organizational charts define clear paths of the reporting hierarchy, the assigning of departments and divisions, and the roles and functions of these units. Organizing formation for employees can be vital to a company. Employees must know their roles and functions, as well as the task that are at hand. Providing employees with an organizational chart gives them a road map of who to contact or speak with and can help managers and employees in achieving organizational success. It also cuts down on time management when employees know and understand the structure of the organization, their role of the organization, and who to report to if they have any questions or concerns.

If managers plan to achieve organizational goals, it is imperative they have some type of **control** system in place. Managers must monitor what it is they are trying to accomplish. They must put forth their best effort to strategize the best solutions in problem solving to create goals that will meet the needs of the bigger picture of an organization. They must make changes and adjustments a long the way when they see anything hindering the effect of reaching the goals of the organization or their unit.

As a manager in a **leadership** position it is imperative that you oversee the operations of the workforce effectively.

A manager is a title that can display leadership qualities. Not all managers make good leaders. However, in this role of leadership and management it is someone who can provide guidance and direction to his or her employees. One of the first skills to learn is to lead and direct employees. Instead of seeing yourself as a boss, consider yourself a leader. A manager with good interpersonal skills can enhance the quality of employees work and increase the organizations productivity.

Be A Role Model

As a manager you want to identify what it is you would like to accomplish in your new role. Take a moment to reflect back and ask yourself a few questions. "What do I want to convey to others? What do I want to stand for? How will my role impact others around me and the company I work for? "What legacy would I like to leave in my leadership position? How will I go about accomplishing these task?

In a leadership position and being a manager, **you will be portrayed to someone as a role model.** You may never know whose life it is you could have an impact upon. As you meet people along your path you may affect someone's successes or failures, goals and ambitions, or hopes and dreams. You do not have to be an entertainer, political figure, or movie star with all the fame and publicity that goes in that world. In fact, your role is much more personal because you are in constant contact with people around you. You may affect someone by the decisions you make, the actions you take, or the messages you deliver. Whether they are your superiors, subordinates, or colleagues, your actions are being noticed. Whoever it may be, someone is always watching you, so always try to lead in a positive direction.

When leading, one of the driving forces that come to the forefront is what we value. One of the issues people in leadership roles or in power do not realize is when they are managing people or an organization what they value can be the driving force of their forethought to the organization and the workforce. In other words, the things that you value that are important to you may be displayed as important to the organization.

For instance, if you value honesty, you may look at integrity as being important, or if you believe in always doing the right thing, ethics may be what you value. If you believe in hard work, that may also be what you value and portray to others. So ask yourself-what do you value most within yourself? What is important to you within the organization? Take some time to let your mind absorb some of these thoughts. Give yourself a moment to reflect back on your beliefs, values, and morals. How can you contribute these attributes into your role? What is it you would like to accomplish or instill in others?

Levels of Management

There are different levels of supervision in management and **each level has a defined role.** The three levels that are defined in this book are top level, middle, and first line supervision [which I consider the beginning of management].

In a management position you are always in the middle. If you are a first line supervisor, you answer to your direct reports and your manager, if you are a middle manager, being in the middle means you are between your superiors and your subordinates, and you answer to both. If you are an executive you answer to a Board of Directors, Stakeholders, Stockholders, or someone of that level.

The top level management is the senior or executive level. They have a higher level of planning within the organization. Examples of top level managers are Chief Executive Officers (CEO), Chief Operating Officer (COO), and members of the executive team such as the Department Heads. They are responsible for the overall operations of the organization. Top level managers think strategically, they focus on long term issues of the organization as a whole. Their focus is in the survival and growth of the organization. They set the tone for the vision, mission, values, goals, and organizational culture of the organization.

Middle level management is below top level and just above front line. Their level of planning is drilling down the top levels strategic plans into a lesser time frame making them tactical. Examples of middle managers are Division Managers or in some cases Senior leadership positions. They are usually in charge of a unit or division. Middle managers report to department heads, or someone at the executive level. They receive direction and guidance from the top. Middle managers are known as tactical managers because they are responsible of translating the executive plans into shorter timeframes and articulating the information to the employees who report to them, which are frontline managers.

Frontline managers are your lower level managers, usually known as supervisors. They work directly with the workforce. They are the link between management and non-management. Their mission is to carry out the tactical plan to make it operational. First line managers make the operational plan the day to day operations of the workforce, which is critical to the organization.

One of the ways to make the organizations plans successful at any level is by providing the plans to the employees, along with setting some expectations for employees. Expectations should be given at every level of the organization.

EXPECTATIONS

Expectations tell what is expected of an employee. It is utilized as a roadmap. It provides direction and guidance telling employees what road to follow. If employees know what to expect, they will know how to reach their goals.

Let's **imagine getting on an airplane and not knowing the destination.** First, would you get on an airplane not knowing its destination? For most people this is a scary thought; they would not do it. Not knowing which direction you are traveling or where you are going can be a bit frightening and uncomfortable. Think of your employees, they could feel the same way.

Consider this, what is the first thing a flight attendant does before the plane takes off? They go over the flight emergency plans in case something should happen. They are basically giving you the airlines expectations of what they need from each passenger if something should happen. Imagine if something did happen, and these expectations were not covered. The plane would be in complete chaos during an emergency and no one would survive.

Well consider your employees the same way. It may not be as critical as an airplane emergency, but you can see the difference if someone knows in advance what is expected of them compared to not knowing at all. As a leader always provide expectations to your employees. Expectations should be written for all employees. They do not have to be long and lengthy, you can make your expectations simple by writing them in **RASS** form

- **R**easonable – being logical and fair when writing expectations
- **A**ttainable – employees should be able to achieve their expectations
- **S**imple – easy to understand
- **S**pecific – direct instructions of what is expected

Expectations do not have to be hard and complex. They can be straight to the point. Keep it simple for everyone to understand. Use simple words staying away from hard or difficult words. When writing, keep your writing at a level readers can comprehend. Complex words may be hard for readers to understand or time consuming to conceive (i.e. having to look up words in a dictionary). Easy reading is more appropriate.

If you do not provide expectations to employees some employees will have no idea of what you want or what you expect of them. Tell employees your expectations. This will make your job at least 90% easier. When writing expectations, do not just write expectations, explain them to everyone. Never assume that people may know or understand what you are asking. Once you have written your expectations, have a meeting with all of your employees discussing these expectations. The meeting should be in the beginning of your leadership role.. You can also use your expectations and incorporate them into a mission statement, or part of a mission statement.

Provided on the next page are employee expectations from a call center.

EMPLOYEE EXPECATIONS

Productivity: Quality Customer Service is our first priority. Ensure telephones are answered immediately and professionalism is always displayed.

Policies and Procedures: Everyone should be knowledgeable of the call centers policies and procedures.

Attendance: Everyone is required to maintain a good attendance rating according to policy guidelines. (*if no policy is enforced you may want to create one or indicate rating definitions)

Staff Meetings: To ensure staff meetings are productive all staff meetings are mandatory.

Integrity: Always be honest with our internal and external customers.

Courtesy: Ensure courtesy & professionalism are demonstrated and practiced at all times.

Training: I encourage and support all of you to enhance your skills and solicit training where you deem necessary.

Timecards: All timecards should be completed by the end of each work day. It is the employee's responsibility to have timecards completed and checked for accuracy prior to turning them in to a supervisor at the end of the week.

I expect everyone to follow the rules and regulations of the organization, adhere to the expectations, and work as a team to achieve our goal of providing quality service to the customers we serve. If you should have any questions or concerns, please feel free to see me.

Supervisor Name
Supervisor Signature

If I were an employee looking at these expectations I would know what you expect of me. In viewing these expectations I would know what you expect from training, professionalism, and productivity. I would also know I could come to you if I have any questions. The roadmap is there; it is very plain and simple. Once you have completed the expectations read them to yourself. How do they sound?

Are they **R A S S** ™ - **R**easonable, **A**ttainable, **S**imple, and **S**pecific?

Questions to ask to begin the expectation list:

a. What are your expectations of me?

b. What is your definition of an excellent employee?

c. How would you like me to address critical issues with you?

d. How will I know if I am not meeting your expectations

Now you are ready to write your boss' expectations. What kind of expectations could you possibly give to your boss? Ask yourself what do you expect from your boss. Use the **RASS** theory when writing your expectations. An example has been provided for you on the following page.

If you had the opportunity to write expectations for your boss, what would you write. What kind of expectations could you possibly give to your boss? Ask yourself what do you expect from your boss. Take a few moments and think of some expectations. Use the RASS theory and write them down. Would they look like these expectations.

Expectations of My Boss

- Lead by example in a positive manner
- Respect my thoughts and ideas
- Mentor and support me through my career path
- Be flexible and adaptable to change
- Be fair and impartial to all employees
- Keep me informed of current situations
- Let employees be responsible for their area of responsibility
- Let me know when I do something right
- Let me know in private if I do something wrong
- Follow the organizational values, mission, and culture
- Empower employees for career growth by creating opportunities for employees to gain skills and experience

Take the example above from the boss expectations. Would your boss be able to live up to these expectations? If you believe so then you have just written what you expect of yourself. These are the standards that you are willing to live by as a leader. These are now *"your new"* expectations. Place them somewhere you can always refer back to now and then as a reminder of the kind of leader that you want to be.

You can also perform the boss expectations exercise with your employees. Have the employees write down expectations of what they think makes an outstanding employee. Do not let them know they are writing their own expectations. Once they have completed the assignment let them know what they have done. Advise them they have written their own expectations for them to live by and strive for.

Organizational Culture

Organizational and Corporate Culture are used interchangeably.

Culture is defined as shared characteristics of values, beliefs, customs, norms, ways of thinking, or traditions. It is a key set of common perception and shared meaning by members of the organization.

Organizational culture helps to define what the organization represents. It is the routine behaviors, the tangible signs/ artifacts, norms, values and characteristics of what the organization stands for. The organizational culture drives the organization and its actions. It can foster a control mechanism for employee behavior, how employees think, act and feel. It is lead by the vision, mission, values and beliefs of an organization, usually set by its founders or leaders of the organization.

The tone of the organization can be sensed by: the written and unwritten rules, the rules of the game for getting along, the things you see and don't see. Organizational culture can and does have direct affects on employee behaviors and performance. Organizational Culture can drive motivation in a company. The unwritten rules are the rules that are unwritten within the organization but everyone is aware of them. You may have a rule regarding lunch times and hours, but you may see people taking extended time and it is being accepted. It becomes the unwritten rule because it is not written anywhere but everyone can see it. No one says anything until usually someone is being discipline for it or a new leader comes on board. And what happens when the leader comes on board.

The famous saying comes out "We've always done it that way".

I've heard many stories of organizational culture, and how the culture rewards certain individuals. For example, if someone makes recommendations or suggestions to improve the company or product, they are usually the one handed down the task of getting it done; whether they want it or not. After a while, the person will no longer make recommendations because their reward is more work. So the culture is adding more work to employees who try to make suggestions instead of acting upon the idea and giving it to another employee who would welcome the idea and challenge. Or what about the employee who makes all the noise and gets rewarded? What are the patterns of behavior that are acceptable in your company?

Vision

The **vision** forecast the future of the organization. It is a starting point of creativity. It is someone seeing something and creating it in their mind. A vision becomes the future because it is seen beyond today. A vision is important because it provides everyone within the organization an end result. If the vision of the organization is shared with employees, everyone can see the direction the organization is heading

Mission Statement

A mission statement tells why your organization exists; your organizational purpose. It is telling how the organization plans to accomplish a goal, task, or project.

<u>Values and Beliefs</u>

Values are the organizations belief system, the ethics and conduct of the organization. **Beliefs** are the principle or idea; one considers to be absolute truth. Values and beliefs are important because they display character. They tell people about you, who you are, what you believe; It describes you and the type of organization you believe in operating. Values influence attitudes and behaviors. It can tell what is acceptable or unacceptable in an organization. Share your values with customers and employees. Let them know who you are and what the organizational values are.

Empowering Employees

Empowering employees is one of the best rewards you can give to an employee or the organization. Give employees an opportunity to let their light shine. Provide an atmosphere that encourages employees to establish intrapreneurial ventures. Intrapreneurial is having the freedom and empowerment to manage another persons business as if it were their own. Let your employees brainstorm their own ideas to improve the business. Employees who participate in the development of a project tend to take ownership of their work. When it comes to the functional or technical aspects of the job employees can be your best consultants.

Empowered employees make decisions, take ownership, solve their own problems, and become intraprenuerials. You don't have to own a business to make decisions or feel a part of the business. Empowerment allows employees to make decisions at the lowest possible level, but still have the opportunity to seek help or advice when needed.

Encourage employees to take on new challenges and new ideas. You as a leader can have a better "buy in" from your employees if they have the choice in ownership. Pick employees who want the responsibility or are willing to accept the responsibility. Try to match the person with the project. Once you have assigned the employee a project, coach them through it teaching them all the aspects of the project, or depending on the circumstances of the project give employees the latitude to make decisions and take charge.

Some employees may not want the responsibility of being empowered or innovative, so be careful when selecting employees. You as a leader should observe the employees searching for ones who would be good leaders. When we decide to empower employees we are letting them make decisions. All employees are not on the same level so each may require something different.

Example: Have you ever been to a department store where you had a small problem that you thought any employee could handle. Let's say for example it is exchanging or returning an item. The employee assisting you informs you they are not allowed to make return or exchange decisions and they must seek a manager's approval.

While they go to get the manager you wait another five minutes. When the manager arrives they instantly approve your transaction. Could we have saved your time and the manager's time by empowering the employee to make that decision? I am sure we could have. Empowering employees and allowing them to problem solve is good for growth, good for business, and good for employee morale.

Be flexible to change within your organization. Give employees the empowerment to be creative and do the project their way. You may have a certain way of how you like to get things done. The employee may understand your way, but may have a better way of handling the assignment. Let the employee try it their way, it may be better. What you want is a **positive end result**. There is more then one way of handling issues or situations.

Example: You have a certain way of how you file folders. The employee may have another way of filing folders. It may not be your way, but it will still get the job done and have your positive end results.

If an employee can think of a way to do the job effectively to benefit everyone, including the organization, you have just empowered that employee. You have given the green light to say it is okay to make decisions and think of new ideas. Employees want to be a part of an organization; they want to feel valued. Employees want to be a part of the organization and have a feeling of the sense of belonging and of self worth. Many researchers speak upon these issues of people's needs.

Theories of Psychologist

Motivating Employees

American psychologist Abraham Maslow (1908-1970) speaks about the theory of people. He developed a theory of motivation describing the process by which people progress from basic needs to self-actualization. Maslow's hierarchy of needs is listed as follows:

Maslow's Hierarchy of Needs

SELF ACTUALIZATION

ESTEEM NEEDS

SOCIAL NEEDS

SAFETY NEEDS

PHYSIOLOGICAL

Self-Actualization: To find self-fulfillment and reach one's full potential. It is the top of the line of achievement. It a self-satisfying inner need to achieve a goal. Something that will be self-satisfying to that person. When people have a specialty that they are yearning to accomplish, they have a need to succeed or feel whole in their accomplishment.

According to Maslow this need is never really satisfied and not many people reach this need. In this need, people are always looking for more for satisfaction.

Employers can meet these needs by: Developing employees, helping them reach their full potential by giving them projects or assignments that will challenge them. Allowing employees to do something they desire.

Esteem: Internal and external self esteem-having a sense of self-respect and respect from others; to feel valued; recognized.

Employers can meet these needs by: Recognizing employees for their achievements, giving employees meaningful task, and asking employees their opinion.

Social Need-Belonging; to feel accepted; to affiliate with others; to have friends to give and receive love and affection; to be cared about, and not being alienated

Employers can meet these needs by: Assigning team projects, having social gatherings (potlucks, company events and picnics) for employees to get the chance to meet other workers, and to provide a sense of community within the organization.

Safety is the need to feel safe and secure and free from harm; to be in an environment free from danger; to be economically secure

Employers can meet these needs by: Providing a safe working environment for employees, and offering them job security by less lay offs as possible.

Physiological Needs are survival needs. These are the things we do to meet the standards of living, i.e. having water and food to nourish our body, needing air to breathe, having shelter for us to stay, and receiving medical care. These are basic survival needs humans need in order to survive.

Employers can meet these needs by: Providing lunch breaks for employees, significant breaks between work hours (usually two 15 minutes breaks are sufficient) providing employees the income to purchase their standard needs of food and water and basic living, and providing a healthy clean work environment for employees.

Maslow hierarchy of needs is in a triangle setting starting with the lower-level needs at the bottom. Maslow theory is that once a need is met, the person will move up the triangle to the next need. The first four mentioned are known as deficiency needs. Everyone will have different needs and they will be categorized differently. First come survival needs (based on above chart). For example, starving people will take greater risks to obtain food. Once they have accomplished or fulfilled that need, they will move on to another need, like safety.

Maslow's hierarchy shows people have different ranges of needs from survival to self-actualization. The lower level needs are usually basic needs which must be fulfilled before reaching higher level needs, such as esteem or self-actualization.

ERG Theory

Clayton Alderfer of Yale University reworked Maslow's theory and named it the **ERG theory.** Alderfer argues that there are three core groups of needs where people can be motivated on all three levels. These core groups are: **E**xistence ,**R**elatedness, and **G**rowth; labeled **ERG.**

Existence	Concerned with providing basic material existence requirements. This aligns with Maslows physiological and safety needs.
Relatedness	Desire we have for maintaining important interpersonal relationships. This aligns with Maslows social and external esteem needs.
Growth	Desire for personal development. This aligns with Maslows self- actualization and internal esteem needs.

Studies have shown that the middle levels of Maslow's theory tend to overlap, which Alderfer has collapsed into three levels. Alderfer theory demonstrates that more than one need may be operative at the same time, and if the gratification of a higher level need is stifled, the desire to satisfy a lower level need increases. For example, if growth opportunities are not met, the individual may reflect back on relatedness needs until growth opportunities can be met. As managers, recognizing these behaviors will help in meeting employee needs.

The **ERG theory** recognizes that all three need categories can be operating simultaneously, where in Maslow's theory a lower need must be gratified before one can move forward. Like Maslow, Alderfer ERG theory has the hierarchical needs where existence needs have priority over relatedness, and over growth. Alderfer ERG theory allows the order of needs to be different for different people.

ERG theory also contains a frustration-regression dimension. Alderfer explains that when a higher order need level is unfulfilled, the person may regress to lower level needs that appear easier to satisfy. So the frustration can lead to regression to a lower need.

Achievement Motivation Theory X

David McClelland studied the need of motivation theory. He believed that people had an intense need to achieve. The need to achieve is a personality characteristic. David McClelland theories of needs of motivation are as follows: McClelland is best-known for his research on achievement motivation, his research interests ranged from personality to consciousness he developed the scoring system for the *Thematic Apperception* Test which was used in achievement motivation research. Later, he became interested in the relationship between achievement motivation and economic development. Before his death, he conducted research on physiological influences on achievement motivation. McClelland's concept of achievement motivation is also related to Herzberg's motivation-hygiene theory. People with high achievement motivation tend to be interested in the motivators (the job itself).

Need for achievement: The drive to excel, to achieve in relation to a set of standards, to strive to succeed. The need for achievement is the desire to do something better or more efficiently than it has been done before. High achievers differentiate themselves from others by their desire to do things better. High achievers are not gamblers; they dislike succeeding by chance. They prefer the challenge of working at a problem and accepting the personal responsibility of success or failure.

Need for power: The need to make others behave in a way they would not have behaved otherwise. The desire to have impact, to be influential, and to control others. Individuals enjoy being in charge, strive for influence over others, prefer to be in competitive and status- oriented situations, and tend to be more concerned with prestige and gaining influence over others than effective performance.

Need of affiliation: The desire for friendly and close interpersonal relationships.

The desire to be liked and accepted by others. Prefer cooperative situations rather than competitive ones, desire relationships involving a high degree of mutual understanding.

Delegating Projects to Employees

Delegating projects to employees provides opportunities and growth for employees to develop their skills. When delegating projects or responsibilities to employees be specific by telling the employee what you expect as an end result; include deadlines when delegating assignments. Always give yourself and the employee enough time to complete the task.

Example: It's November 1st. If you have a project that is due to your boss December 1, have the employee meet their deadline by November 15. This way, you will have enough time to review the project prior to it being submitted. Never give deadlines where the employee does not have enough time to complete the project or make corrections on the project.

There are times when there is not enough elapse time for the project. Be sure to give it to an employee who can handle this deadline. You may want to delegate this project to an employee who is familiar with the project, or one who needs little supervision to get the job done, and has a history of completing projects with good results. One thing I would not recommend is giving it to an employee whose work history you are not familiar with.

Once you have given an employee an assignment make a log of it. Put it in your planner or on an office calendar. This way you have the dates available to you, when the project was assigned, the project due date, and the employee in charge of the project. You can also create a log in your computer with this same information. Either way is fine, whatever is convenient for you is what counts.

When you delegate assignments, tell the employee how you would like them to report back to you. If it is a new employee and you are not familiar with their work you may want them to report to you once or twice a week, depending on the assignment.

If it is an assignment that is complicated you may want to give it to an employee whose work you are familiar with. You can possibly have them report back to you once every two weeks or once a month, again depending on the assignment. Whatever the assignment may be always set follow up dates to meet with the employee(s). During these follow up meetings you can see how the employee is progressing. This will also give you a chance to review their work and coach them through when needed.

If you delegate an assignment to an employee and they seem to be unsure about what they are doing, go back and see if your instructions and objectives where clear. Set up a meeting with the employee to make sure they understood the assignment given to them. If necessary, review the instructions again and give the employee assistance to give them a head start. It may be best to have the employee repeat your instructions for understanding or possibly provide examples or guide them through what you expect as an end result. This way, any misunderstanding or miscommunication can be addressed in the meeting. Be sure to have follow up dates with the employee to clear any future confusion. You will not have to do this all the time, it usually occurs with employees on new assignments or where you are not familiar with the employee's work history.

When assigning a project to an employee, let the employee know the reason why they were chosen to handle the assignment in the first place. You must have felt comfortable in giving them the assignment and felt they could complete it and do an outstanding job. This in itself should build the employees' confidence level to go ahead and complete the task.

In the beginning, most employees may not feel comfortable with empowerment and decision-making. It may be something that is very new to them. They may feel uneasy because they are doing a project for the boss. In the beginning of your delegation and giving out your expectations, it is important that all instructions are clear. You can also write down or tape record your instructions so the employee may have something to refer back to. This will keep the employee from coming to you with detailed updates. With written instructions, the reassurance of them doing the job correctly is on paper.

In the beginning it may take a lot of your time, but what we must focus on is the end result. Soon you will be able to delegate priority tasks or projects and you will be able to depend on that employee because you have coached them through other projects.

Example: I use to belong to a gym where they did not empower their employees. On my first visit to the gym I waited thirty minutes for a manager to give me a tour. Only the managers were allowed to sign up new members and provide tours to guests of the gym. While I was waiting for a manager a few of the employees were standing around the reception area talking. I asked if one of them could sign me up and give me a tour. The employee at the desk stated that only managers are allowed to show tours and sign up new guest.

So in the meantime, I waited another fifth teen minutes until it was my turn for the manager to give me a tour.

Once I went through the tour, I could not see what was so hard about giving the tour. I waited until the manager was finished with the tour before I asked any questions. I asked the manager if their employees where knowledgeable with their equipment and able to handle tours. The manager answered, "Yes they are, they are required to go through a training course for gym equipment and learn about the facilities, just as the managers. Next came the burning question, "Are they capable of providing tours to guests and new members. The manager answered, "Oh yes, quite so, but it is company policy to have the manager provide the tours and sign up new members. It has always been that way.

How many times have you heard that? *"It has always been that way."* Do not let that be the rule of your organization. Throw out the old way of doing things and let fresh new ideas help your organization. Be unorthodox, do something different, let your company stand out. Old procedures do not empower employees to reach their best potential or to be part of the organization.

Mistakes are Bound to Happen

When coaching employees keep an open mind and allow room for mistakes. Learning from mistakes gives employees growth and experience. How else will they learn the functions of the assignment or position if they are not allowed to make errors?

The mistake can only be a growing experience for that employee. Do not chastise or discipline the employee for their mistake. Show them how to improve from their mistakes and do not assume everyone thinks like you do. Be flexible to change, everyone has a different view of how to get things done. Remember, the person doing the job may not do it as well in the beginning, or as well as you, however, with coaching and assistance they will become better at it. Do not forget to recognize the talents of your employees and compliment your employees on their assignments.

When innovating and empowering your employees enlighten them and strengthen them to become better employees. No one is saying give your employees a huge project and expect them to be great at it! Give employees baby steps and with your assistance and coaching, show them their true potential. Give them small projects to achieve what could eventually lead to big projects. Empower your employees to be a part of the business, a part of the vision, and most of all, a part of a team.

Let your employees feel confident that you and the organization value their contributions. Let them know what they are doing is important to the business. This is very important because it will build confidence in that employee. Remember mistakes are going to be made, and a lesson is going to be learned, so give them the room to grow and make mistakes, and compliment them for their achievements.

Reward your employees by showing them you recognize their achievements. With today's technology you can print a certificate from your office computer, praise them in front of their peers, or put a nice letter in their file. There are many ways to reward employees without spending a lot of time or money.

There are many different trends to rewarding employees. For instance, employee of the month, employee of the quarter, or employee of the year. Either of these you could choose from, the choice is yours. Basically, the point is the employee who does extraordinary work is receiving an award. Match the awards to their achievements.

I have seen plaques in many work places. Plaques made with star of the month, employee of the month, or achiever of the month, with employees' name and/or picture on the plaque. You can create your own employee title for your organizational plaque.

Example: I worked in a place where their profession was to save lives. A supervisor bought a few bags of lifesaver candy and made some certificate cards that read "thank you for being a life saver". They glued the lifesaver to the paper and distributed to all the employees.

There are many ways to recognize and appreciate employees. Most times, a pat on the back or acknowledgement of good work is simple enough.

Making Decisions

Decision-making is the conscious effort of making choices. We decide on a daily basis different choices that affect our lives. When it comes to making choices, we determine through the alternatives that are given to us, what choice we are willing to accept, and we call it making decisions. When making decisions, managers may use different types or styles of decision-making.

- ✓ **Decision by authority**
    - o The person who has the power to make the decision
- ✓ **Decision by minority**
    - o Small group of employees exert their influence over the majority
- ✓ **The Democratic process**
    - o Majority rules-people with the most votes
- ✓ **Decision by consensus**
    - o Finding a solution that is acceptable to all members
- ✓ **Decision by unanimity**
    - o When all members are in full agreement

IMPACT MODEL

Problem solving is looking at a situation and figuring out the best solution to the problem. It is good to have an **IMPACT**™ on your problem solving skills. The **IMPACT** theory is a model to assist with problem solving. It can be used for performance improvement plans, career development, strategic planning, or daily living activities.

IMPACT

I identify the problem/issue

M measure

P plan

A action

C change

T timing

I-Identify the problem/issue

<u>Gather the facts</u>

- What is the problem/issue?

- Who does it involve? affect? (stakeholders, public, organization, employee (s)

- When did it happen?-timeframe?

- Where did it happen? (on/off company property)

- Why did it happen?

- What was the cause?

- How was it discovered? (internal/external)

- How will the ones involved be impacted?

- How can it be solved?

Solving the problem-Developing the solution

- What solutions can solve the problem?

- Have more then one solution, start with the best one?

- Who will it impact?

- What will it solve?

    – Will it solve it directly/indirectly

    – Band-aid approach

    – Short term/Long term fix

M-Measure-make it measurable

How will we know we are successful?

- Measurable-make it measurable
    - o What will you measure to know if it is successful
    - o You want to measure what you are trying to accomplish
    - o How are we going to measure it
    - o What tools or resources do we have available to measure our plan
    - o Plan goals and objectives

P-Planning is everything

- **Put the solution into a plan**
    - – Plan on what you need to accomplish to make this happen
    - – What tools & resources do we "need" to make our plan effective?
    - – Research the plan
    - – read, meet with people, network
    - – see what has already been accomplished
    - – what was successful and what wasn't

Plan on what you need to accomplish to make this happen. What do you need to make your plan effective? Research your plan through reading, meeting/ networking with people who have already accomplished this task. Look at how others did it, was it successful for them?

A – Action-put your plan into action, and monitor your plan for change(s).

- A-action-act upon those plans-are they working

C – Change: Be prepared to make changes

- What changes need to be made to improve the plan
- Most successful plans have made many changes before they were perfect. Successful planning requires flexibility. Be flexible to change until you get it right

T – Timing is everything:

- Provide a timeline for your plan.
- How long will it take you to succeed with your plan? Give yourself a deadline and stick with it.
- is this the right time to implement this process

IMPLEMENTING CHANGE

Many organizations are changing the way they do business. Whether it is for customer service, new technology, or training, most employees do not adapt well to change. History has shown that people fear and resent what they do not know or understand. When implementing changes within an organization, seek input from employees and provide communication of the changes taking place. Employees should be part of the change process. They should be allowed to provide input to their employer regarding changes. Research as shown employees who have some type of involvement with the change process seem to adapt better. Being involved helps staff adapt and can encourage "buy in'. Remember, human resources are your best assets. Employees know what is needed to make their job function in an efficient and cost effective manor. They are "free" consultants to your organization.

The majority of these employees have already discovered how to create shortcuts, decrease production cost, or increase sales. Gathering input from your employees is wise and is more cost effective than hiring external consultants. Do not get me wrong, consultants serve a purpose, however, you can obtain much needed information from your employees as well.

Some organizations will hire outside consultants and spend thousands of dollars to hear from someone who has no clue about the organization or its culture; when they have their very own consultants within the organization. Employers should ask the employees, seek information from employees who do the work on a routine basis, and are familiar with the culture.

Employees appreciate it when managers are open to employee's suggestions. Allowing employees to express their ideas invites the employee to feel that their opinion matters. When we invite input and listen to concerns and suggestions from employees we try to implement those suggestions into the organization. However, for many reasons there are some suggestions that cannot be implemented. When issues like this occur, explain to the employee the reason why the change could not take place. If it is financial reasons, policies, or just not feasible, tell the employee. If it is a matter that cannot be discussed, tell them it can't be discussed and don't discuss it. Whatever you do, do not embellish on the reasons but always be truthful. Employees will respect you a lot more for telling the truth. They may not always agree with your answer or the reason, however, they will be more open to understanding. People tend to accept things better when you are honest. Anytime you can, and if time permits, take time to explain why the change did not take place without releasing important or critical information.

Consultants can be conducive to any organization. However, if organizations provide guidelines to "their" employees of what they want to accomplish and empower the employees to make decisions, they will find that the organization will have a much more productive pool of staff than they could ever imagine. Employees want to do a good job, they want to do research, head committees, and gather information to complete a project. Unfortunately, some employers would rather pay outsiders the high cost of consulting fees. The benefits of consulting with employees is cost effectiveness, encourages employee involvement, and employee commitment.

When conducting business with employees it should create a "We" partnership. "We" is the key word that shows teamwork and team collaboration. Ask the employees what can "we" do to make "our" organization more effective and productive. These words show inclusion, and states we are all part of one team. Use this approach and see how many great ideas come to mind from your staff!

Employees who get involved may feel they have a buy in with the organization, and a sense of ownership within the company. You do not have to be an entrepreneur to feel ownership of a business. You can feel ownership with someone else' business or within your own organization as an "**intrapreneur**" (having the empowerment of operating another person's business, using your skills, talent, and experience). Let employees have empowerment to run a project or assignment. Let their innovation come up with ideas that would better the company. Let employees take risks just as you once did.

Taking risks is very precarious, however, you are not taking the chance of going out of business or letting your working capitol run low. I am simply suggesting to employers to let your employees be creative without being fearful of making mistakes.

Most employees have idea's that are cost effective to save the company money (i.e., a policy change of doing business more productively, a new way to boost morale, or a new concept to save money). Whatever the change is let the employee use their mind to make it work. You can monitor the progress and if you are not sure if the program will be successful you can create a **pilot program.**

A pilot program is a trial period to test a certain product, a change, or an idea within a certain time frame. The program is then evaluated at a later date to see if it would be beneficial to the organization. **For example**: Let's say your organization will test a software change to see if it will be advantageous to the corporation. The trial period will be for 30 days. If the idea works, you can implement the change into the organization. If it doesn't, you have not lost anything but the employee has gained your trust. They will feel that you believe in their ability to think, be creative, and to be part of the organization. But most of all, you have built self-confidence in the employee to perform their duties to their best abilities.

I do not believe there are employees who want to do badly within their job performance or organization. Good employees are like gems. So when you have good people of great treasure, treat them as such! The true measurements of good employees are hard to find, but most good employees are right under your nose. Could you imagine if you had an organization full of treasured innovative employees? I would think you would be the next Bill Gates, a millionaire.

The bottom line is treating your employees with respect. Let their imagination and creativity flow to enhance your business. Reward those employees with praises and perks when they take risks, instead of punishments and discipline. Celebrate the successes of the employees who add benefits or profits to your organization. Let the workplace be a positive place to work and grow.

When an employee has a complaint

When an employee has an issue and they bring it to your attention acknowledge the employee's issue. The worse thing you could do is to ignore it. Validate the employee's complaint by letting them know you are concerned and you will look into the situation. If it is something you will be able to provide feedback, let the employee know you will get back to them within a certain time frame. With some complaints you cannot tell the employee the outcome but you can let them know the issue will be handled. If it is feasible, ask the employee what they would like done. Most of the time they just want the situation handled.

When a complaint is brought to your attention <u>check all the facts first</u>. I cannot stress this enough. This means investigate the complaint. Do not assume everything you hear is true. *There are three sides to every story*. The complainant's side, the accused side, and then the truth. Your job is to find the truth. Question the involved parties and gather statements and information. In what ever you do document, document, document. Write your information then evaluate the facts and statements before you make a decision.

When making a decision stay objective and always be fair and impartial. Make your decision on the facts you have gathered. Do not make a decision on emotion; you will regret it later. Sometimes observing the situation before you react can also be a decision. But whatever you do, do not ignore it. If discipline should become involved never tell the other employee(s) that the accused employee is being disciplined for their actions.

Remember the saying "*actions speak louder than words*". If you have to discipline an employee the disciplined employee's first actions must have been noticeable to employees, therefore, their second actions will be noticeable as well. In other words, other employees should see a difference. Sometimes this is not always the case, however, the actions will show up in the end if you follow through with your discipline procedures or the employee may reach the final destination of job termination. It usually does not get this far, however, if you should reach this point with discipline procedures, then these problems have most likely occurred all along and action is finally being taken.

Supervising Friends

Supervising friends can be a difficult situation, especially if these friends are also your previous co-workers. You would think most friends would respect you in your new position. While this may be true to some degree, most friends will feel they can get away with a lot more now that you are the new boss. When you are friends with your previous co-workers immediately establish ground rules. Balance your supervisory role and your personal relationship between your profession and friends.

The best way to handle this situation is to establish rules of expectations. Remember to stay fair and impartial with friends who are subordinates. Give everyone equal treatment and treat *everyone* the same. Discuss your expectations in a team setting so everyone can hear your message. Let employees know what you will expect of them and what they can expect from you.

Do not discuss any other expectations with friends because the rules should apply to everyone. Your actions and impartial ways should send a clear message to everyone, including your friends. Remember those expectations you wrote earlier? Now is the time to give them to your staff. Let them know what you are going to be expecting from them and provide them the roadmap to get there.

If your friends still choose to speak to you about the matter be open and honest about your standards and your decision. As a supervisor remember to be yourself, becoming a supervisor for some can become overwhelming. As a friend, let your friends know that you respect them and you will always be fair and impartial. You will not make decisions on friendship, but on ethics and integrity alone. Let them know you want to do your best as a leader and you would like their support, they can only respect you for it. Keep in mind, most friends have your best interest at heart, so they do not want to jeopardize your career or your friendship. If they do – were they ever really your friends to begin with?

What happen to friends when something does not go their way?

What happens when friends are supportive until something does not go their way or they are being disciplined? This being the case, remember to concentrate on the facts and do not let your emotions lead you. This is why it is important to establish expectations in the beginning; so friends understand your role as a leader, not as a friend. Your primary role is to be a leader, who leads by example, and to remain fair and impartial under the circumstances.

Previous Co-workers who resent your new Position

When previous co-workers resent your new position never feed into or buy into an ex-coworker's resentment. Treat the resentful employee like any other employee on the team. If the person does a good job and you would normally tell the employee, tell it to this employee. If their performance needs improvement and you need to tell them, tell them that too.

If necessary, have a meeting with the resentful employee to resolve any issues the employee is experiencing. Usually when an employee is confronted with these issues they tend to change their ways. This does not hold true for everyone so you must use other alternatives if the employee is not open for discussion. However, the sooner you discuss the relationship the sooner you will have a better understanding of what to expect from each other.

Dealing with difficult employees

Dealing with difficult employees can be hard and time consuming. They can make your job more complicated than what you want it to be. Employees can be difficult for many reasons: not showing up for work on time, always calling in sick, not being a team player, or being a malcontent about everything and everybody. Did I mention anyone you might know?

These employees can have a negative impact on the rest of the team or the organization. Depending on the problem and the severity of the situation, have a one on one discussion with the employee. Be firm with your expectations. If you have an employee who has performance problems let the employee know your performance standards and what is expected of them. Give the employee performance ratings if necessary.

Discipline

When is discipline necessary? Discipline comes into action when an employee violates a policy or procedure and the supervisor feels it is necessary to document the violation as a discipline. A supervisor can document an incident without it being deemed as disciplinary whether it is for corrective action or governing conduct. Discipline should be handled at the lowest possible level. However, it can escalate if the employee does not improve their behavior or action. Discipline is basically trying to change a negative behavior that would hopefully have positive results through corrective action taken to improve the employees' performance or behavior.

When we have to discipline an employee it is usually not the best part of our job. However, in any leadership position, there comes a time when it will most likely happen. When providing discipline to an employee clearly state the problem. Let the employee know what policy was violated. If possible, provide the employee with a copy of the policy that was in violation.

Discipline decisions can be tough. I encourage you to be creative and use your own mind when making decisions. Focus on the problem and not the person. When we discipline employees we are looking for positive end results; to correct the problem. Stay objective to what is best for the employee and the organization. Once you have made your decision be consistent and stick to it.

Leaders who cannot make up their mind about a discipline procedure do not give accreditation to what they are doing. Be prepared when giving discipline, have the paperwork with you, and know what you are going to say. It will help during the process.

Being in this position is not easy, and being a leader does not always bring us glory. As the leader, you are expected to put out fires, and keep them out, and the ones you cannot keep out, you will be expected to control. After all, you are the leader, and that is part of your job.

When disciplining employees remember this one simple rule: ***treat others how you would like to be treated***. When you are dealing with a situation that may be conflicting or it makes you feel uneasy, take some time to get your thought process together and take personal involvement out. If you need to go through a thought process or time to yourself, do it before approaching the involved employee. Then look at the situation as a problem. Ask yourself "What is the problem?" What did the employee do? What rule was broken? Compare the problem to the rules and regulations book. Most employees know the rules and regulations, and they know when they are violating the rules. A few may not be aware of the rules they are violating; however, we will give them the benefit of doubt.

Never go into a situation accusing an employee. Ask the employee if they are aware they are violating a rule. Be sure to have the regulations with you so you can point out the violation to the employee. Once you have shown it to the employee, make sure they understand the rules and regulations. This is so you hopefully will not have to be in this position again with this employee.

When dealing with conflict or discipline, earn your AA (Ask before Accusing). You do not have to go to school to earn an AA. Human kindness and respect is in the heart and not learned in school. Next time you must handle a situation, remember your AA, Ask before Accusing.

Be specific- let them know what rule they have violated. Most employees do not like or appreciate beating around the bush. Do not forget this is an adult you are talking with. Once you have established there is a violation, listen to what the employee has to say. Give them a chance to tell their side if they need to. It may not change anything, but most times employees are more receptive and it makes your job easier.

Always approach a situation with tact. Try not to be on the defensive. Remember that you are not the problem, you are merely addressing the problem. Remain objective; remember you are not the judge and the jury. Your duty is to remain impartial, look at the situations and facts, and help resolve the problem with a viable solution. Never approach a problem or situation and leave it unresolved.

When it comes to discipline documentation is important. There are two types of documentation provided for you. One is a documented counseling which could be considered as an informal discipline in some organizations. The other one is a corrective action letter, which is usually, considered a written warning. It provides documentation that the employee has been informed about their action or behavior with out it being considered any type of discipline. The most common form used is the documented counseling, however, I would use the corrective action form first if the situation were not serious

The documented counseling is a counseling session you have with the employee regarding a corrective action that needs to be documented. The documentation is the discussion of the counseling and the planned outcome.

Is there a best way to discipline employees? I don't know if there is a best way to discipline employees. No employee wants to receive discipline, nor does any supervisor want to administer discipline. Disciplining employees is very tough; however, it is part of the job when it becomes necessary. When you are going to discipline an employee because of their behavior or performance talk to them in private. Do not discipline an employee in front of their peers or the work place. Anytime an employee is going to be spoken with about their negative behavior or performance, it should always be in a private setting.

When counseling employees for discipline treat people how you want to be treated. Do not demean the employee for their actions. Speak to the employee about the problem. Obtain feedback from the employee about their actions. Try to help the employee with viable solutions to correct the problem. Most employees want to do right, so once something is brought to their attention they try to fix it by correcting their error. Give the employee time to correct their problem.

You can also try to work with the employee utilizing the IMPACT theory to develop a strategy to improve the employee's performance. The IMPACT theory will allow the employee to set goals and set forth an effort to improve their behavior, actions, or performance. You would be the mentor or leader to assist the employee with this plan.

Also, know the difference between a "need" to discipline and a mistake. Errors are going to happen, employees will make mistakes. So be careful to identify the two before putting pen to paper. When employees make mistakes give them room to grow, especially if it is a new assignment. This is called training and mentoring. You are assisting the employee to develop new skills.

If an employee makes an error that must be documented use it as a training tool. Advise the employee of their error, provide a solution or a better way to handle it, discuss with the employee so they have an understanding of how they can correct the problem.

Documentation or discipline is to make the employee a better employee. It is to hopefully change the employee's behavior and not to punish or destroy the employee. Remember that these employees are your assets, they are very valuable. If you destroy them at your organization, another organization will see their potential and let their light shine and reap all the benefits of what your organization could have had.

IMPACT EXAMPLE:

I   Tardiness-having problems arriving to work on time Solution: to be at work ten minute early each day

    1.   Set alarm clock 15 minute forward
    2.   Leave home 10 minutes earlier
    3.   Get a good night sleep so I can wake up refresh in the morning

M   Will measure plan at the end of each week and review tardy record to see if Jane Doe is complying with the tardy policy.

P   Jane Doe will also have a friend call her 15 minutes after her alarm clock should go off to make sure she is out of bed and preparing for work. This process will continue for 30 days.

A   Plan will begin immediately and after 15 days, we will review the plan to see if it is working

C   No changes needed at this time since still in infant stage.

T   Plan will be completed within 30 days (date)

Agreement: These are the terms and conditions the mentor/ employee agree upon when they are in their initial meeting.

Mentor and Jane Doe will meet each Friday 30 minutes prior to closing time to review Jane Doe tardy record. At the end of 30 days, Ms. Doe will be re-evaluated to determine the duration of the program and if improvement has occurred. If no improvement has occurred, Ms. Doe is aware that disciplinary action will be taken against her and could lead to termination.

Comments:

_____

_____

_____

_____

_____

Name   **Date**   **Supervisor**   **Date**

Company Name

TO: **Division file of (employee name)**

Date:

Employee Rank/Title

FROM: **Supervisors Name**
Rank/Title

SUBJECT: CORRECTIVE ACTION NOTICE

This is a corrective notice informing you of an area that needs improvement. This is not a disciplinary action, however, it could serve as a foundation of such if your action is repeated and the problem does not resolve from this day forward.

Area needing correcting or improvement:

State the area that needs correcting

Policy or reference being violated:

State the policy or rule being violated

Employee Signature (optional)   **Date**

Company Name

TO: The Division file of (employee name)   Date

From: Supervisor Name
             Title

Subject: **Documented Counseling**

On (date and time incident occurred) you were in violation of policy (policy number) which states (copy policy information).

Describe in detail what the employee did to violate the policy, include dates, times, places, names. Whatever is needed to provide a clear picture to the employee and other supervisors if they needed to read this documentation.

Describe what remedy was given to the employee to correct the problem.

Employee Signature (optional)   Date

Checklist of handling employee problems

1. State the problem or situation

2. Explain how it conflicts with policy (provide copy of policy-optional)

3. Ask employee to comply with policy

4. Explain further action will be taken with discipline

5. Document the situation (if needed)

6. Monitor the situation to ensure it does not continue

7. Bring a positive note to the employee attention (after monitoring the situation and the situation has been corrected, advise the employee you appreciate their compliance. This also lets the employee know the supervisor was paying attention)

Example-Employee not complying to the grooming standards

☐ Problem: Grooming standards not being followed

☐ State why or what is out of compliance-example clothing

☐ Explain the policy of grooming regarding the proper clothing attire

☐ Advise the employee to comply with the policy

☐ Advise the employee if they do not comply further action will be taken

☐ Document the situation

☐ Monitor the situation

☐ Make positive note to employee if it does not continue

Attendance Evaluation

Attendance evaluations are also important. If an employee is not reliable and does not show up for work, how are you as a supervisor suppose to handle this problem? Some organizations do not provide attendance evaluations; however, if your organization has an attendance policy in effect you can utilize their policy as a guideline to measure an employee's attendance.

Most organizations face attendance problems when they provide paid sick leave to their employees. Organizations who do not offer any sick pay do not always incur this problem because employees do not get paid for sick time. Employees who use sick time are usually taking vacation time, other paid time, or Absent Without Pay (AWOP). However the case, employees with poor attendance problems need to be addressed. If you have an employee with a poor attendance problem you may want to use the attendance form provided for you. The attendance form can be the beginning of your documentation advising the employee there is a problem.

As a leader, you may want to help the employee with goals or solutions to resolve the problem. You can use the aforementioned goals brought up in the previous chapters or the IMPACT theory to assist the employee in resolving the issue. The goal is to help the employee improve in their attendance and report to work.

When evaluating an employee's attendance, you have four ratings to choose from (i.e. Excellent, Satisfactory, Improvement needed, and Unsatisfactory). If your company offers sick leave benefits, it would be wise to implement a policy or guideline to rate employees absenteeism on a consistent basis.

Even though situations vary and you would need to use your own judgment that works best for you and your organization. The key to attendance evaluations is to keep the employees on track and help them be reliable and dependable in showing up for work.

Your Company Name Here			
Division (optional)			
Employee's Attendance Review			

Employee Name		Title	
Date		Supervisor	
From	To	Quarter	

ATTENDANCE RATING			
Excellent	**Satisfactory**	**Improvement Needed**	**Unsatisfactory**
Comments			

TARDINESS RATING			
Excellent	Satisfactory	Improvement Needed	Unsatisfactory
Comments			
Signature:			

Performance Appraisals

A performance appraisal is a written document to let the employee know how their performance standards are progressing. It gives the employee a reference of how the company views their work performance. It also gives the employee a chance to establish goals to improve in areas where needed.

Performance appraisals help employees become better employees. Good leaders will manage their employee's performance, provide feedback to the employee, give solutions for improvement, and provide continual contact with the employee to see how their goals are being met. Performance appraisals can be reviewed every three, six, nine, or twelve months, depending on the organization, employee, or leader. Use the appraisals to recognize strengths, accomplishments, and areas of improvement.

When giving an employee their review have the employee expectations and job description with you (* job description- a written statement of what a jobholder does, how it is done, and why it is done). If an employee works in a higher classification then their normal assignment, have that job description available as well. Discuss achievements, goals, and improvements; appraisals should be a mutual conversation agreeing to terms of improvements and goals, however, the supervisor would have the final say.

Performance appraisals are used as learning tools to help the employee. Never ever give an employee discipline during an appraisal, or tell them, for the first time, of an incident they did wrong a long time ago. This is done totally separate from an appraisal. As these incidences occur, employees should be notified. However, if the incident happened within the performance appraisal time limit, then it can be included. But, I will caution you on how to use it.

Example:

Six months ago you disciplined an employee for their attendance and since the discipline the employee has improved. Write it in the appraisal to show the employee you noticed their improvement.

> **Punctual:** *There has been great improvement with Ms. Employee's attendance. Her dependability is an asset to our organization.*

You did not mention the discipline, but you did let the employee know you have noticed an improvement and their dependability is a contribution to the organization.

Employee(s) need to know if they are meeting or exceeding the company's standards. Provide performance appraisals for your employees on a regular basis.

Appraisals come in many different forms depending on the company. Most appraisals have a rating system on different performance objectives. Some appraisals are comprehensive usually with a performance heading and a narrative of the employees' performance. If your organization does not have performance appraisals create a document and provide performance appraisals to your employees. There are different ways to evaluate or appraise employees. You can use the formats illustrated in Appendix A.

The performance rating form is a good form to use for "peer to peer", "boss to subordinate", "subordinate to boss", or "employee self-rating". It does not take a lot of time like the comprehensive evaluation.

Peer-to-Peer evaluations are good to use where peers or co-workers can evaluate each other. This tool is most effective because peer pressure has always been the common ground of getting peers to address their actions, whether positive or negative.

The evaluating peer should have the option of signing the evaluation or remaining anonymous. The key is to evaluate their peer fair and impartially. Most peers remain anonymous because of work pressure or future resentment. The beauty of peer-to-peer appraisals is that peers work with each other on a daily basis so they are familiar with their co-workers performance.

A supervisor should review the evaluation prior to giving it to the receiving subordinate. Each evaluation should provide constructive feedback, and not used as a peer bashing session. This is why supervisors should always read the forms prior to meeting with the employees. Be careful to explain the rules to the subordinates so they clearly understand their objectives in evaluating their peers.

Boss to Subordinate is your standard protocol of evaluations where a supervisor evaluates their subordinates. A good suggestion would be to gather input from other supervisors regarding the employee's performance (if the supervisors have working knowledge of the employee's performance). This would give the supervisor evaluating the subordinate a clear picture of how others perceive this employee and how the employee should be evaluated. This also provides input and inclusion from other supervisors who observe the employee on a daily basis.

When rating employees, have the employee rate themselves first, then compare your rating with the employee, and then discuss. This will create an open dialogue for discussion. It will let you see how the employee views himself or herself, and it will help the employee identify key areas to work on. This appraisal is usually very effective for employees because they tend to rate themselves harder then the rater.

Subordinate to Boss provides employees a chance to evaluate their superiors. Most supervisors do not like this technique, however, if they look at it in a positive manner, the evaluation will let them know if they are meeting the needs of their subordinates. With the subordinate to boss situation you can add or edit the evaluation to indicate mentorship, leadership, or vision of the organization as a rating for the boss. Ratings that would not apply to the boss in the original appraisal rating can be edited with other ratings.

Providing Constructive Feedback

When providing feedback to employees you want it to be constructive. Feedback must be given where employees can take the opportunity to receive the feedback that will assist them in developing their skills, and allowing the employee time to work on those new skills. Below are different models and techniques in providing constructive feedback.

Feedback characteristics

☐ Provide information in small dosage. Allow the receiver to process what you are saying.

☐ Be descriptive and provide examples for clarification

☐ Support the information with sources or recent examples

☐ Allow the receiver to control the information

☐ Ask for solutions or ask open ended questions regarding how the receiver can deliver or contribute to the organization

Sandwich Model

Models for constructive feedback

When using the sandwich approach, tell them what they are doing well, provide them with areas of improvement or your concern, and end on a positive note of working to make things better.

☐ Before your meeting write down 3-5 things you appreciate about the person

☐ Write your concerns and why they are your concerns

☐ Engage in conversation of how the concerns can be improved by providing or asking for suggestions.

Using the model above, think of a situation where you can use this approach to provide constructive feedback.

_____

_____

_____

_____

_____

_____

Goal Setting

Goals give us focus. It provides us with a course of action of achieving accomplishments. Goals give us a systematic way to help monitor progress, evaluate situations, and make improvements when needed. It can help individuals take charge of their lives by overcoming obstacles, barriers, and self-esteem issues. Goals can help one to believe in themselves, their abilities, and their belief that they can move toward higher echelons. People who are successful in their lives are invariably goal setters. They have an action plan and set goals to achieve them. Goal setters know what they want and they know how to achieve their accomplishments.

When setting goals you want to be specific in what you would like to accomplish. Goals that are too broad will not give a clear picture of the roadmap you are trying to follow. You want to follow your goals in the same way you would follow directions. For example, if you were to read instructions from a cake box and follow those instructions as directed, you would accomplish making a wonderful delicious cake. Well, the same holds true for written instructions for goal setting.

Setting goals help you measure your success by looking at where you are now and tracking your record toward where you are heading. Let's say you would like to be skilled in computer technology. The software you would like to learn consists of six courses, as you complete each goal mark your success.

Set a deadline as to when the goal should be completed. Be sure the goals and deadlines are realistic. You would not set a goal to lose twenty pounds in one week. This goal is unhealthy, impossible and not realistic. You want to consider all factors when making goals and meeting deadlines.

For example: You are working forty hours a week, and you have a family you must also provide attention to. You would like to attend school to learn about computer software, however, realistically, you may not be able to achieve this goal in three months. When setting goals with time specifications, keep in mind other activities that take up your time. So in this example, it may be realistic to set the goal for nine months instead of three months, to provide time to deal with other issues as they arise.

Now you are ready to sit down and write your own goals or to sit with your employees and help them establish goals. There is a career goal worksheet you can use as an example in on the next page. Remember when setting goals with your employee's goal setting is a mutual conversation with the employee leading the conversation about their ambition and dreams. You are there to simply provide guidance and support to assist the employee in reaching their goals.

Each goal the employee accomplishes will build self-esteem and provide them a since of confidence in their abilities. It will also fill your organization with confident, ambitious, productive employees who are willing to achieve and take on new challenges.

SMART Goals

S   Specific-must tell what needs to be accomplished

M   Measurable-must be easily measured

A   Attainable-must not be to difficult or easy

R   Relevant-must relate to organizational goals

T   Time bound-must be guided by a specific time frame

_____

_____

_____

_____

_____

_____

_____

Self-Development Chart	
Success of Tomorrow Depends on the Preparation you make Today	
Name	**Date**
My goals I would like to accomplish are:	**I plan to accomplish these goals by:**
1.	1.
2.	2.
3	3.
	Deadline:
My goals I would like to accomplish are:	**I plan to accomplish these goals by:**
1.	1.
2.	2.
3	3.
	Deadline:
My goals I would like to accomplish are:	**I plan to accomplish these goals by:**
1.	1.
2	2.
3	3.
	Deadline:

Career Development Chart			
Time Frame	**Goal**	**Action**	**Deadline**
Short Range			0-1 year
1			
2			
3			
Long Range			1-5 years
1			
2			

Appendix A

Sample I

Performance Appraisal

<table>
<tr><td colspan="4" align="center">Organization Name
Annual Performance Review</td></tr>
<tr><td colspan="2">Employee Name</td><td colspan="2">Date</td></tr>
<tr><td colspan="2">Classification</td><td colspan="2">Review period</td></tr>
<tr><td colspan="2">Supervisor</td><td colspan="2">Dept</td></tr>
<tr><td colspan="4"></td></tr>
<tr><td>E</td><td>Excellent</td><td colspan="2">Consistently exceeds job standards producing superior results</td></tr>
<tr><td>A</td><td>Acceptable</td><td colspan="2">Performance meets job standards</td></tr>
<tr><td>I</td><td>Improvement needed</td><td colspan="2">While performance meets job standards, some improvement is required</td></tr>
<tr><td>U</td><td>Unacceptable</td><td colspan="2">Performance is not meeting minimum job standards</td></tr>
<tr><td colspan="4"></td></tr>
<tr><td colspan="4">Supervisor Comments:

</td></tr>
</table>

PERFORMANCE CATEGORIES				
	E	A	I	U
Adheres to the Organization Mission, Value, Vision Statement				
Follows Department Policies and Procedures				
Leads by Example				
Interacts with internal/external customers in a professional manner				
Team Player-help other team members without being asked				
Requires minimal direction or supervision				
Makes appropriate decisions and takes action when appropriate				
Complies with performance procedures				
Utilizes resources to enhance skills and knowledge				
Accepts constructive feedback regarding work performance				
Knowledgeable using company equipment				
Displays a respectful, cooperative and positive attitude				
Displays a spirit of teamwork				
Has a positive attitude towards the job and co-workers				
Customer Service Oriented				
Punctual arriving to work and from breaks				
Supervisors Comments:				
Appropriately makes decisions and applies the decisions to the vision, mission, values, beliefs, and culture of the organization				

Knowledgeable with current technology				
Reliable-uses small percentage of sick time (sick leave is below company average)				
Applies the values, vision, mission, and corporate culture to daily work ethics				
Interpersonal skills coincide with the organization's culture				
Applies knowledge and experience to new situations and idea's				
Accepts responsibility for his/her actions whether positive/negative				
Knowledgeable in their job duties to perform independently				
Employee strives to work smarter (utilizes shortcuts to get the job done faster)				
Efficient with time management				
Adheres to grooming standards				

Employee Comments:

Performance Appraisal

COMPREHENSIVE PERFORMANCE APPRAISALS

Organization Name

Mission Statement

Yearly Performance Appraisal Report

Employee Name_____ **Date**_____

Classification _____**Dept** _____

Supervisor _____ **Date**_____

E	Excellent	Consistently exceeds job standards producing superior results
A	Acceptable	Performance meets job standards
I	Improvement needed	While performance meets job standards, some improvement is required
U	Unacceptable	Performance is not meeting minimum job standards

Provide narrative statement. Include at least one example in each category

INTERPERSONNEL SKILLS   E A I U

Ms. Employee displays excellent interpersonal skills. She interacts well with co-workers and superiors. She has great customer service skills, as she has received many compliments from internal and external customers regarding her professionalism and courtesy.

ORGANIZATIONAL SKILLS   E A I U

When given a project, Ms. Employee readily accepts responsibility of her work assignments. She has the ability to make independent decisions, and she always meets her deadlines. Ms. Employee work performance got the Nassau Account of 3 million dollars.

DECISION MAKING/PROBLEM SOLVING E A I U

Ms. Employee's problem solving skills are exemplary. While speaking with an upset customer she was able to resolve the problem and keep the customer's account. Ms. Employee has made excellent decisions while taking calls to ensure satisfactory customer service.

LEADERSHIP SKILLS   E A I U

Ms. Employee provides excellent direction to her co-workers and superiors by consistently setting good example to others. She leads by example; she is a hard worker and a dedicated employee.

PERSONAL APPEARANCE   E A I U

Ms. Employee meets and exceeds the company grooming standards.

TRAINING   E A I U

Ms. Employee utilizes her time well. She readily accepts training assignments, follows the training manuals, recognizes problem areas and tries to find effective solutions to solve them, and she provides clear and easy to understand instructions to personnel.

COMMENTS

Rated by_____ Date_____

Peer to Peer Evaluation

Company Name
Division/ Section

EMPLOYEE NAME_____ Title_____

DATE_____ QUARTER_____

List 4 positive attributes about your co-worker (list their best qualities)

1. _____

2. _____

3. _____

4. _____

Improvement Needed: Areas that will help your co-worker be a better employee

1. _____

2. _____

Performance Improvement Plan (PIP)

Conquering challenges is the key to Success
(The affirmation message is optional)

EMPLOYEES NAME .... **TITLE** ....

SUPERVISOR ....

START DATE ....

DURATION: (length of plan)

Area to be improved:

Identify the area the employee needs to improve

How will this be accomplished?

Provide the **IMPACT** theory to set up an action plan

Goals Met

Have the goals of the impact theory been met?

Yes .... **No** ....

Follow up meeting set for: ....

ILLUSTRATION CREDITS

Alderfer, Clayton (1996) "ERG Theory"

Maslow, Abrahm (1996) "Maslows Theory"
"Maslow, Abraham Harold," Microsoft® Encarta® Online
Encyclopedia 2000
http://encarta.msn.com © 1997-2000 Microsoft Corporation.
All rights reserved.

McClelland, David (1996) "Achievement Motivation Theory"

CPSIA information can be obtained at www.ICGtesting.com
Printed in the USA
LVOW11s1538130214

373590LV00004B/976/P